Berth

Megan Stratford

Berth

Megan Stratford

Crystal
Publishing

Fort Collins, Colorado

BERTH

2023 © copyright Megan Stratford
2023 © cover copyright Crystal Publishing, LLC

Edited by Patricia Phillips and Claire Shepherd

Continuous line drawings and cover image licensed from
Shutterstock

Cover design by Deanna Estes, LotusDesign.biz
Interior design by Deanna Estes, LotusDesign.biz

Published by Crystal Publishing, LLC Fort Collins, Colorado

ISBN: 978-1-942624-76-9

Library of Congress Control Number: 2022945130

Printed in the U.S.A.

First Edition

Dedication

For my mom and dad, for their constant
unconditional love.

Preface

Every once in a while, a book comes along that reminds me of how transcendent truly good writing can be, full of wonder and mystery and elegance, against the backdrop of an otherwise cynical age.

We're in a muddled, increasingly angry and increasingly anxious time, no doubt. I guess it's not surprising that much of contemporary creative writing dispenses entirely with old-fashioned notions like Beauty and Truth in the interest of substituting unrelenting Gloom for essential Seriousness. So, I read the collection you now hold with an ever-increasing relief that a kindred spirit is out there, crafting sinuous lines and gorgeous images in the shadow of the Bighorn Mountains out of reverence for something bigger and more enduring than our own immediate angst.

I met Megan once, years ago, at an event in Minneapolis for my own first book, a novel which, funnily enough, is also set in the shadow of the Bighorns. She stuck in my mind because she was kind enough to let me know specifically how much she identified with one of my characters, a young woman of about her own age, heading West to chase a dream. That spot-on gesture meant a lot because it assured me that I'd done something right, created a character "out of my lane" that still rang true to a reader who would know.

Turns out, she herself is also a *writer*, living now and writing about and yearning to know the same Western landscape that inspires a like reverence in so many of us who have chosen this region as home. She composes lines that tap the rhythm not only of syllables and stresses, but of the seasons and cycles and settings of the natural world we inhabit. She sees rock, river, soil, meadowlarks and prairie grass with the eye of a naturalist; she captures wonder with the intuition of a true artist, one who still believes in the sublime notion that both the world and the words to describe it can be beautiful.

This is not to say that everything here is one hundred percent hunky-dory—she hints and intimates and sometimes ruminates on helplessness and tragedy and loss, as any honest life must. Even the land itself can seem like the product of great trial and struggle. *My how ferocious God seems!* she writes, *to split the magma and fossil-stones over and over again with thunder…*

True enough, and we are indeed at the whims and the caprice of forces totally beyond our control. But if that's all we were, prisoners of our own trauma, there would be no concept of the sublime or the magical in the first place, no impulse to create and no dreams to follow, no delight at the way words can be crafted into arcs and whorls to flow into something both lovely and true and so transcend the slings and arrows of merely being alive.

Now here we are, quite a far piece down the road, and I have the honor of cracking the champagne over the bow of this startling, glittering artifact. I can't wait to see what comes next.

Malcolm Brooks
Author of *Painted Horses*
Missoula, Montana

section 1

Unearthing

vellum

I watched as he lumbered from the butte from
the coal escaping its craggy, mucked shroud onto

his vellum, underneath his hook tacks and into
his lungs from weltered fireweed standing
crooked in mountain's crust.

He came, carrying a body
arms legs coiled like a child from marl
child as teal as the slate I skipped with.

Water spills from canyon's crevice
snow spitting her first freeze in October
    an early shower of silver cells.

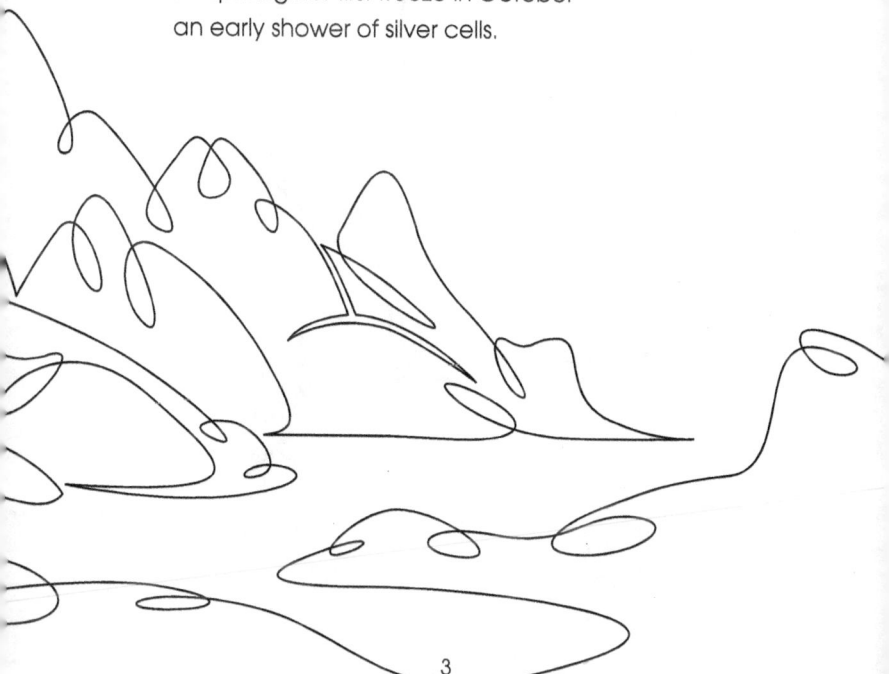

Back Country

hoop necklaces looped with bobbles from back
country's excrement

volcanic ash and ore shaped from loam

weaving lark and locust seedlings made

the prongs stand tall around the pyre

shells that might be drawn from seaboard's ridge

     for they hold language

each of our names chiseled with a sharp mouth

for this wet isle and hoard of pulp is how we came
into order

a wetting

durum yaws along esker's late summer static
a drove of oxen, a wallop of brawny tails over
a swarm of mosquitoes
striving to tipple their trusses dry of blood
argil doing what it does best
bridling the pome
from rot
          from the runaway cutthroat
               from the black-mouthed coyote
staining the air with instinct
       a wetting on the fuzzed
             callow stem

Fracture

All around us are the jagged horns of quarry

A colony of beavers stack their bungalow under
the shoal of aqua glass

The echo of waterfall rumbles more like engine than
the steel-blue swell

Traversing bray & reef

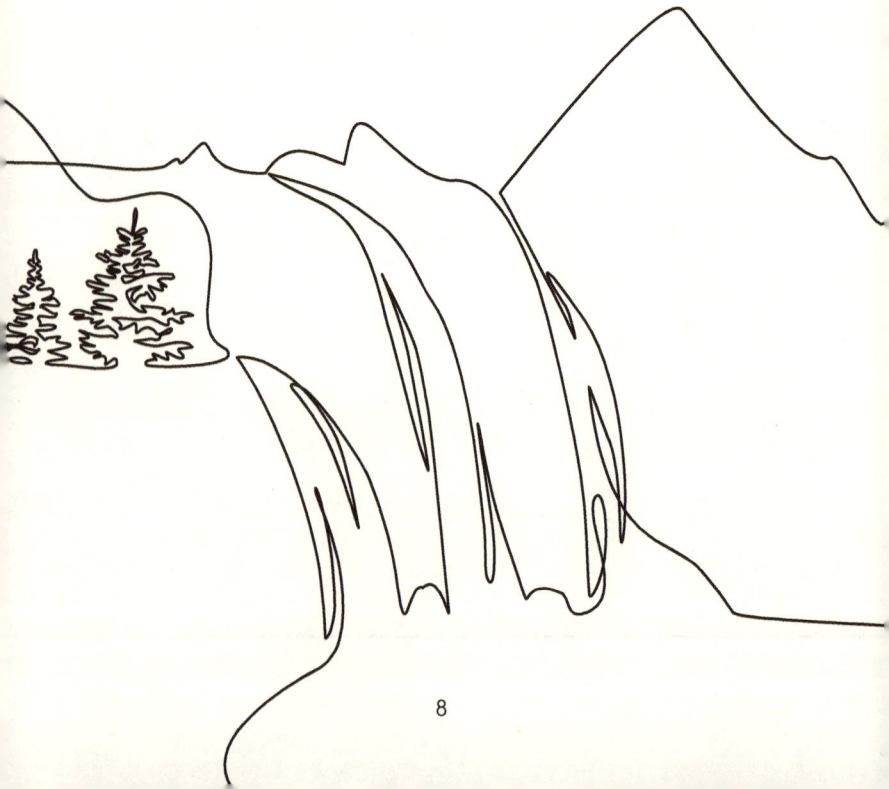

The beetle rimes its own shard
A fracture & zoetic.

In a new shimmery sheath
        A large raven lands & holds together
               The broken bones of cypress.

Oculus

Scrabbling through this winding spire, I am born.

Someone called *mother* shores my head along brute
chaff and swaths my body secure in strips of twill.

I turn loose what I didn't know to be a weapon

A billy club against a brand-new oculus.

Sorting each knot of lilac from your hand
proved hazardous.

We broke the silence with laughter and
watched as water scattered over each
glass ream.

Torrent
rolling around
kitchen slate and bister birdlime.

Coming Apart

i enjoy the taste of earth
        slivers of cream-shaded legumes

parsnip was their family name
        coming apart in my mouth

greenskeeper anchors his harrow like an idol
        shucking the haft with a scrawny peg

jackal skulks across the ice
        across the pond

i wait for something savage to sag into smattered
        water to fossilize the pelt & the clapper claw

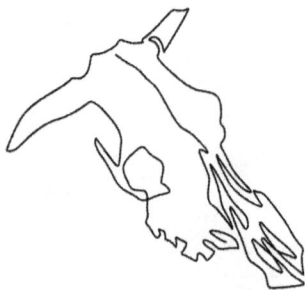

Torment

The moon dips from her sky & onto each pale, blue curl

a tempest's torment

sleeks the slag

gull sculling against its sloshy metar

Now I see that the stag

    standing still on the highway

        keeps me from going

           off the edge

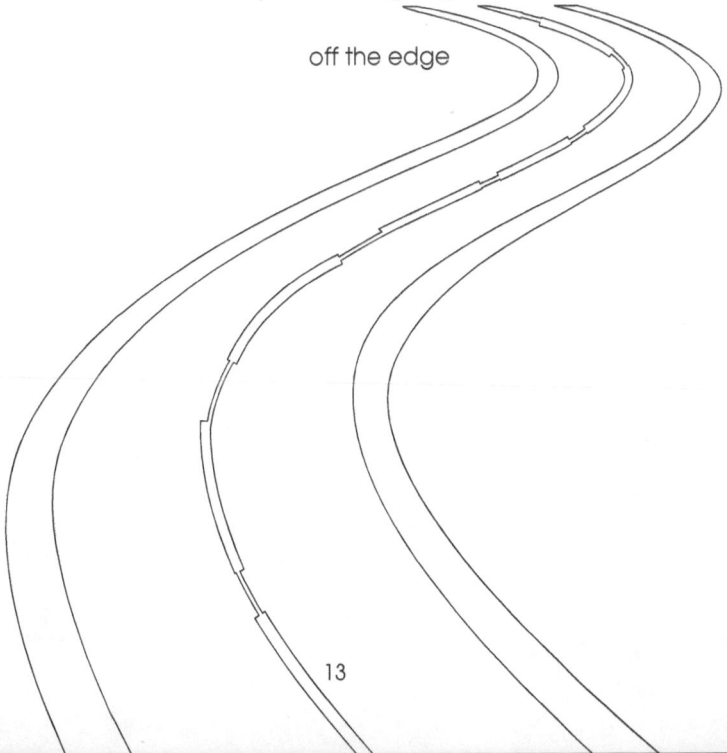

Something Wild

This old sod had been our home

       Where the dust carries itself from the gravel
       road and into the eye of something wild.

A backwood

       Where the tameless straggled throughout
       gilded and gray pastures

       Turned the rivers over with cant hooks
       to unearth a windpipe
       perhaps both sets of ribs from the quarry.

Falling Sideways

All evening I've watched autumn turn
Crystal balls falling sideways from the sky
Riddling Earth's bottom

Sorcerer's high sign curlicue
Draws me in with an invisible rope

This boy I see so clearly is winter
So close by I hear his silence

Boy of salt

Boy of sacrifice

Buck

In sleep
        you walk toward me

tiny alabaster specks
        flurrying from an overcast sky.

We are surrounded
        by the veins of saplings

their limbs crackling
        with the weight of the cold.

The buck
        with leg bent under its own girth

breathes out an ethereal cloud
        waiting for us to remain unstirred.

Bits of His Peel

He unearthed his brother
who had been left to wizen across
a roughened heath for
these sable mornings kept him ripe with dew.

Mosquitoes land on bits of his peel
to suckle what they could get of claret.

For you see
        these sleek coxswains
        cannot be without their sky.

Croon

I stave off the half-aquamarine
half-shadow serpent

where he can slip out of his dead skin
leaving behind a single line of spun-out scales.

You sully braids of sapling, your sweat spittles
skimming both temples.

I listen as you croon throughout the cinder block
and lime and woodlot homestead.

I fasten the gnarled brassknucks of my father inside
the pads of my own slight, coral palms.

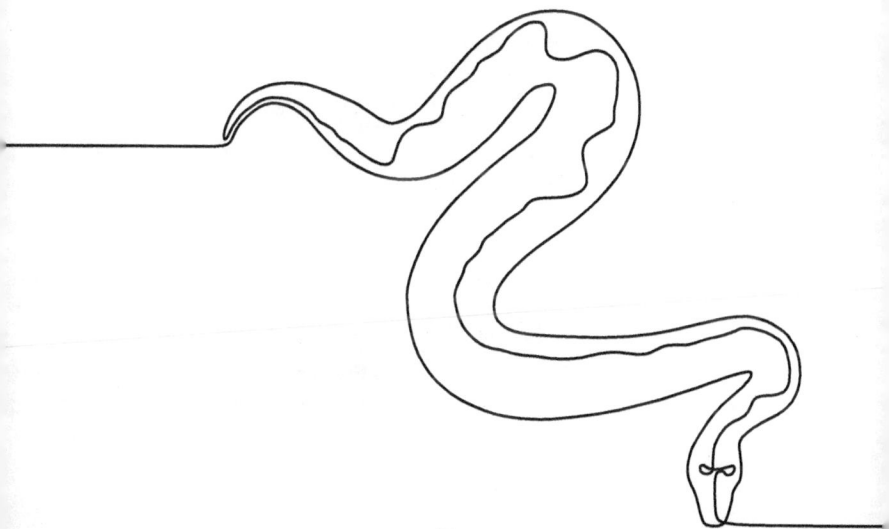

Squall

plead for the ash to disappear from
the billowing flames.

it's only 3 yet the sun turns itself down behind
the bur oak and wingéd elm

which, quite willingly, break their own limbs
standing in the way of a springtide squall.

Gales Shove

I like how winter
opens her smoky splay across a barren flatland
and how the blue spruce slaps back as
gales shove toward the mead.

You won't find the caterpillar turning itself over through
shard and overnight escape its heathery home.

Huntsman aim their muskets at the scad of horned
wildebeest and the racket of
something far off
driven through with tusk and barb.

earth's stain

thicket divides her marrow and red algae equally
before rainwater whelms and wet rots the clay

a rough-hewn dell of burgeon burrows from
earth's stain

tansy ragwort's and golden aster's bottom
harbors something foul

sunrise slides moon into shadow crescent
wakes what is already underneath the zipper of sol

Orb's Brow

The cowpoke's body
was sighted in this very flume
          a face, empty against orb's brow.

I shake the moth
a band of silkened, diaphanous threads from
          the fold of my tunic.

I watch, fuddled, as it flutters toward
          the gleam of embers.

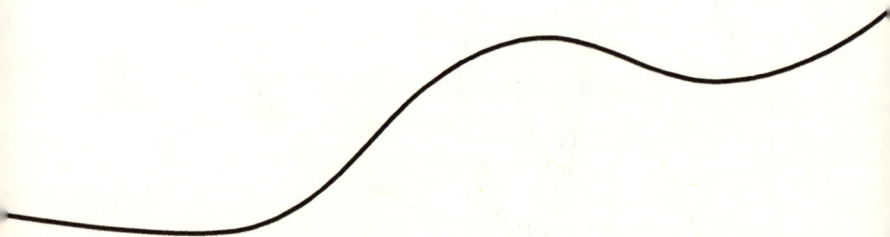

the quiver of saffron

in the openness, a certain contraption rusts.
it grumbles on a low hum for coins

some squat and worn with specks of twine from
    the insides of my pocket.

        we are unaware of
          the other's windedness

        bodies hidden by
          long-limbed tresses.

           I can barely catch
            the quiver of saffron
              in meadowlark's fringe

before
it wears away and I am left
abandoned in the shade of tor.

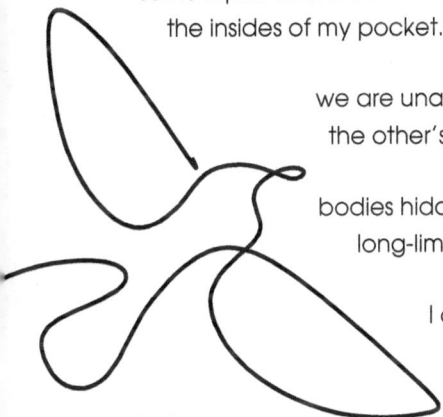

To Have

I listened to night's outburst
as wildwood's mist softened my skin.

I listened for sapling's syrup
to fall in great abundance.

My tongue hoped for something sweet.

I found it best to hold the ground
warming her with my feet.

I cracked open the roaches' shells and
left a trace to say they'd gone.

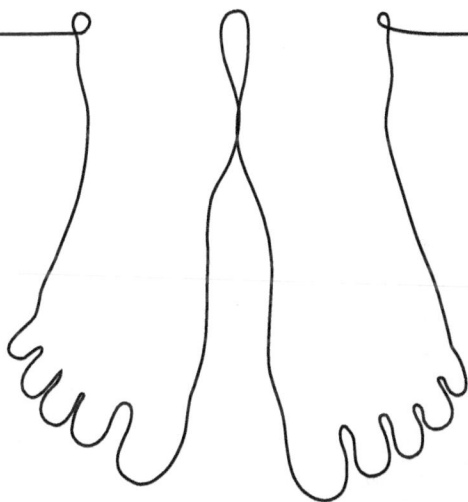

pixie

how would it be to depart inside
a likeness of mine
to climb through the crow's nest's
lanky branches
to swing off and break to the next.

sneezing dandelion's pixie
an angelic's notable afterglow
say you'll be my human for this is glory where you
can you be embraced in creation's bosom.

Blackened Wood

It's hot enough where I can hear the cicadas from
the cluster of trees getting louder

I wait for the uptick, the steady drone of a/c
so I can finally dream

My dad swathes his arms loosely around my neck
pulling me toward him

In slow motion, black bird lands and holds together
the broken bones of cypress

Wings unfurl revealing a velvety shroud
a warning for prowlers who eye for this same spot

Let us pray for the rain
the crops so vehemently demand

Our dog paws at the screen door, waiting to be let
loose into a blackened wood

Waft of Spring

one quivers at looking down
at the stories and stone that would only
keep you from falling any further through
the open waft of spring

rasp a bit more mire
on the stain caused by your own carelessness
while you hold the other palm out for someone
other than me to hold

       you curse greater than my howling

Unclean

i took from the shoreside
whorl shells and jingle shells too

to scrub away the ugliness from the outer rind
        all the way inside
                        me

shells stamped from the swell of the tide and
now the bones of the ocean become part of
                        me

the dilapidated parts of
        someone feral

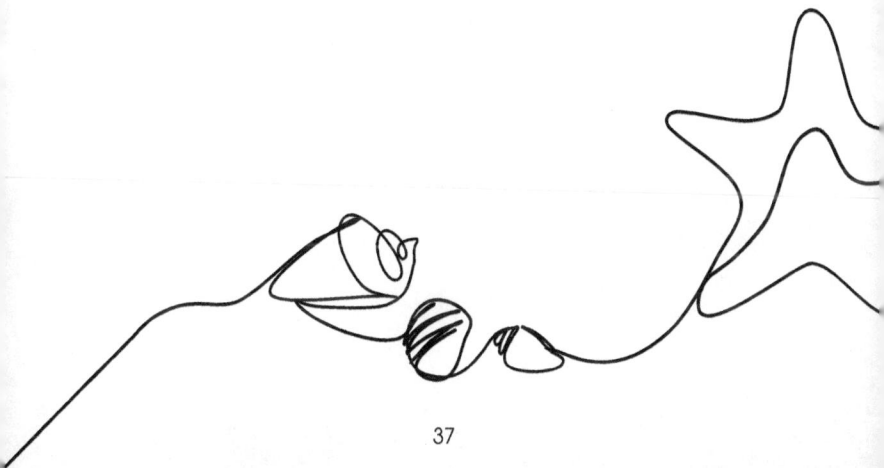

section 2

Rumination

Into the Firehole River

It was sometime during the summer solstice
when I labored waist deep into the Firehole River.

My father said it would be best
to baptize myself in the cerulean-gray oscillations.

The river widened & swerved deep within the prairie
grasses bowing to the tickle of wind
still has me wondering.

That same river swallows my angst
       tosses it down somewhere amidst
             the stones and leaves it there.

where the water plies

Any moment now the dark
will divide the firs in two

sun setting her flame in the riffles
where the water plies and swashes into bedrock.

I sunder from my hand the swirl of rose gold
signifying that at one time I was someone's wife.

The gnarls of coyote
the constant catcalls of Cold Hardy

keep me looking outside toward
the Bighorn's shadowy trace.

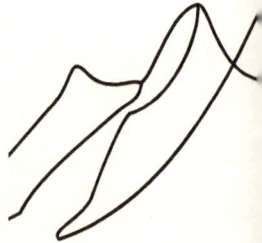

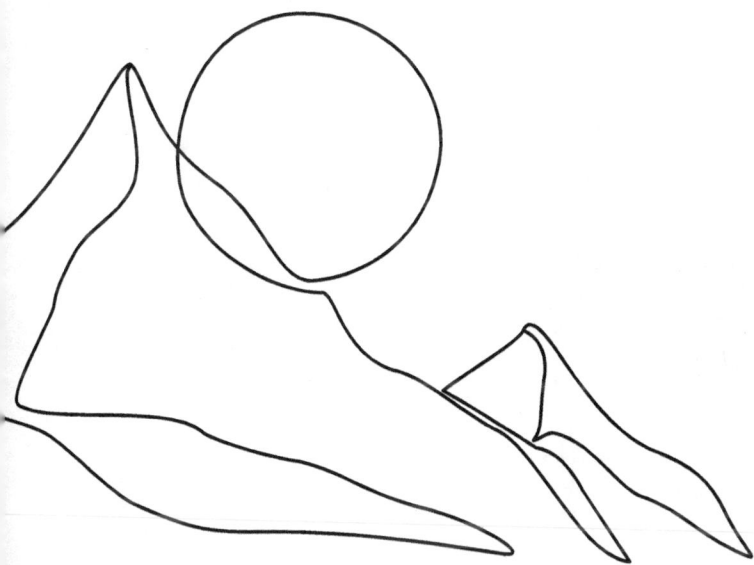

first epoch

Existing in estuary's seam
came memory
first time cradled in your stance.

Casting one hand over the other long ways
like there was a *right* way to catch a fish.

I remember a certain haggard smile
cheek's recessed into the hollow.

Broken-down husk gathering the sweat
spooled from your crown.

This hallowed ground helped me place your
holler as the slippery native
came out like something easily broken.

I tugged while it pulled me back onto the bank

      fella suffocating itself in
      the open.

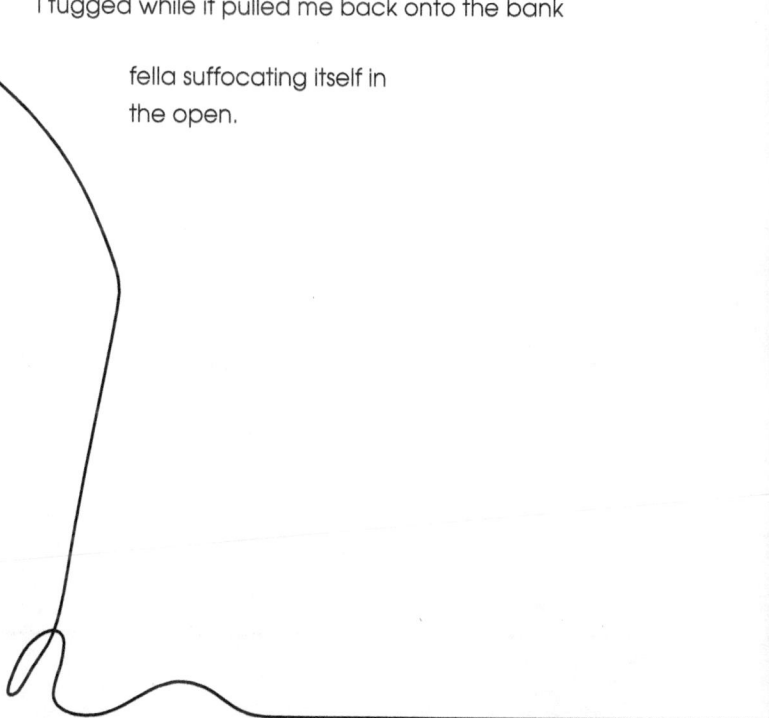

My Mother Splits G_d

each morning my mother splits G_d in half:
land of green pastures and still waters.
she prays each name: Father, Son and Holy Spirit.

she holds them in her palms toward the sky.
its yellow-orange halo takes away her sight
like Saul before he became Paul.

each morning my mother splits G_d in half:
she holds Zion in her palms toward the sky
the promise of everlasting life.

>	her heart has not grown
>	dark, weary or heavy-laden.

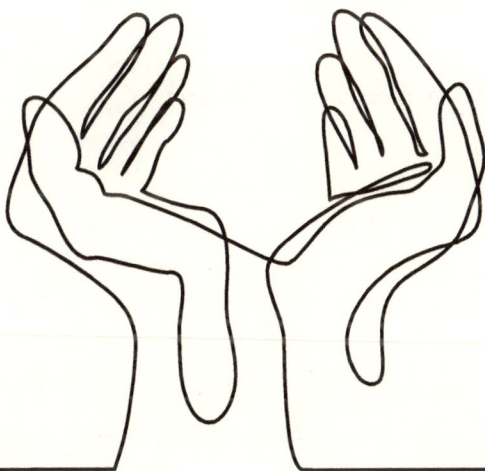

Berth   *for my dad*

This trail you had us ramble
had already been carved through by so many other
hooves

traipsing the yellow-green mosses that much farther
into quaggy sod.

My how ferocious God seems! to split
the magma and fossil-stones over and over
again with thunder.

Out there, the beetle creeps from his shriveled pome
to the pulp of a quaking aspen

a berth where swallow cannot turn up his slick and
sable hull

rifting it wide enough to carry away his heart.

Passage

Few clamor the Beartooth Mountains the way we did
to rumpus the hogan in early black

Go up against the zephyr which licks canvas over us
like a shawl from the nip
your voice crystallizes, taking brief form

Only to disappear amidst the slag amidst
the flame you'd started from birch bark and passage.

My head has fallen heavy against
the earth.

Forgive Me.

For the infant I carry is worming
itself between rib cage and too soon.

It must have been the earth
I'd inhaled to make the unborn depart.

Forgive me.

It wasn't time enough to call him a him

       son in sky or sun and moon

       sun and sunset
           sunrise over the dark

Forgive me.

In the water
when I don't reach out

to save you.

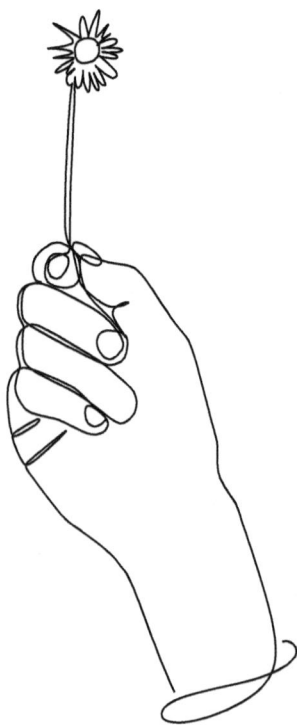

The Back of Him

My father leans his chair back on two legs.
He squints his eyes almost completely shut
shade riding the back of him.

I remember at one time
how i'd braid the stems of
         dandelions
                  a crown of amber.

bitterroot

Daddy beats each hoof
into a certain lip of the bitterroot trail
a fully tipped slab of shale

moldering 'neath the berth of
cannabis
ivory aviators titillate him with their hum

his hand wraps 'round my palm
As if to say
        I am all you need

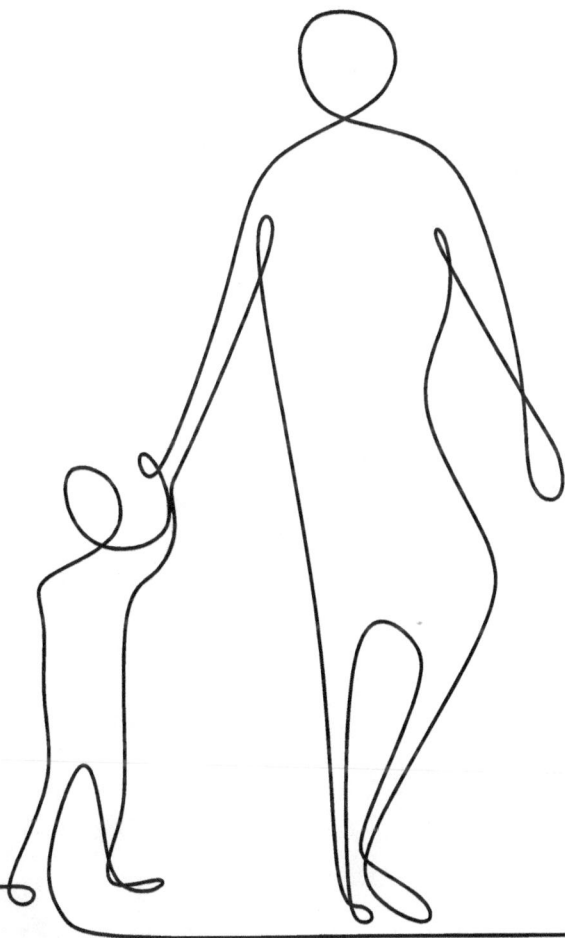

Thru Time

I long to travel thru time

to stumble again, dragging my feet over
the broken stones

       pathways

which swerve into the backyards of strangers.

I wave at those I see
while the other arm pumps fiercely at the open

       air

Cockeyed

He kept me in shadows along
the square-rigged underbelly.

Those who go by a different name
whittle tallies with thumbs

grooves into the frame of lasting another night through
the must of soldier and churn of sea.

I was one of them: amber barked, smacked hard with
crimson scourages.

He had me cockeyed so the thrum of
my heart and skirl of each breath were in earshot.

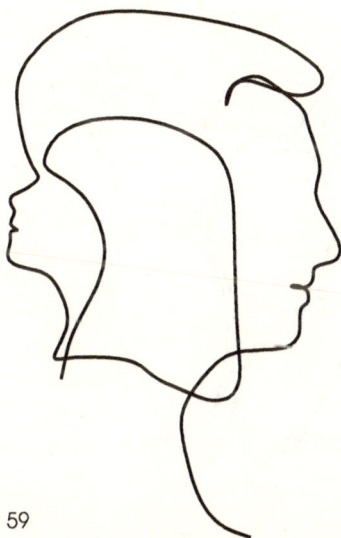

Summer

the wind hurls bits of earth up and down
the dry, narrow riverbed.

new life unfolds on the bodies of cacti
while the sun's
orange-red heat crawls alongside the wild's floor.

men scour the trash bins
pulling from them memory foam and
sheets faded from summer

to sleep amidst
the common sage and date palm underneath
the endless speckle of orbs.

two-harbor lane

north shore's two-harbor lane
is laid out with raw bones

partially unfurled
wild arms reaching wide for sky.

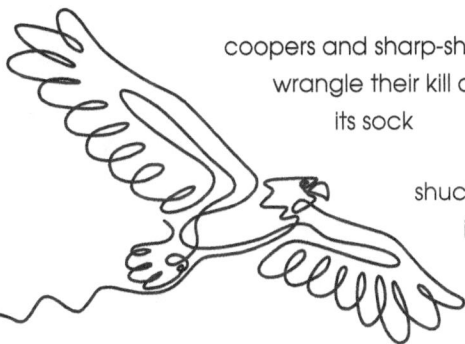

coopers and sharp-shinned hawks
wrangle their kill out of
its sock

shucking the fleece
into cottontails

bits of
down
sailing unpinned

to each orb that had been
picked clean.

section 3

Luminosity

Gravel

They had asked if I had ever tried to take away my life
with my own hands, a tethered shackle of knobby bones
and an undulation of tiny capillaries.

> *Of course not*, I claim.

Bits of gravel lodged from the sleep
that wanted to fold my eyelids over
iris specks.

I had not succumbed to that voice
which had whispered
        I was nothing.

Credence

there was a man who built trellises atop
celestial's finest vantage point

drilling holes through and through panels that wouldn't
hold against hand and rod

steps waned as he inched
leg around terra's scattering spirit

credence catching and then zippering man away on
wonder's wings

>   an ascent into
>   nirvana's prick

bending our bodies

how is it that you continue to dazzle me
hands bending our bodies into curlicue

leg still riding mine
silk against cotton
flesh burning in the same flame

you decide to plant me some place
my rapture might rise so
you would fall and awaken with my blossom
glissading deepest between
the excitement of my thighs

my name is christened in a far-off city

just as the fallen seraph descends capsizing my crux at
one time suitable for glory
today contrived to squirm its way into
me a spirit not that of
the three-in-one Yahweh
Spirit robs me of of time
Spirit withholding claim to
what was rightfully upper G's
   to whisk away on gleaming chariots
   and not be subject to servitude
   belly forth and trespass against
   a night like this

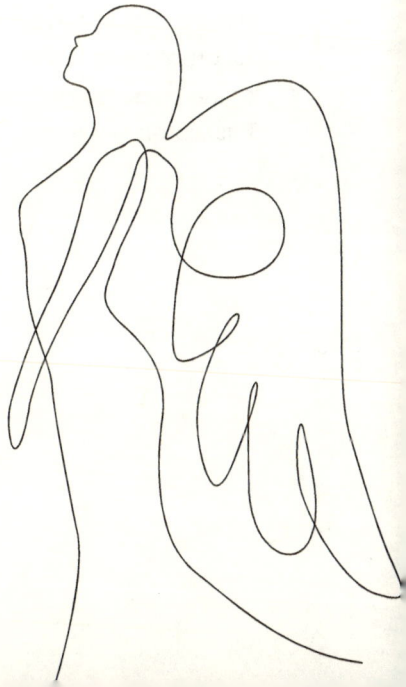

God offers His blessing to twin peaks

straddling its currents & mackerel
rising to the surface which blunders side-to-side
discerning fly from circle of life

seeing beauty best
putting up underneath the muffled hush tones of
offshoots past

fishers of many
quakers of the old west
where everything was left still breathing
even when left to wither its lifetime away in
bigwig's paw

at least populous had time of its life
first breath & its last sigh of relief
for the dead do dance these windriver valleys
& its waters are totem for what God has provided

Future Father

in the beginning
       says he who created the terrain in six days
resting on the seventh to admire it as good
to see it for what it was
            foolproof

lacking a body that had not been formulated through
grit & animation rose husband

future father & without exception nation
superseded son of the almighty providence
brother of no one
rose he
rose he
bare & unashamed overseeing all that was finished in
the beginning

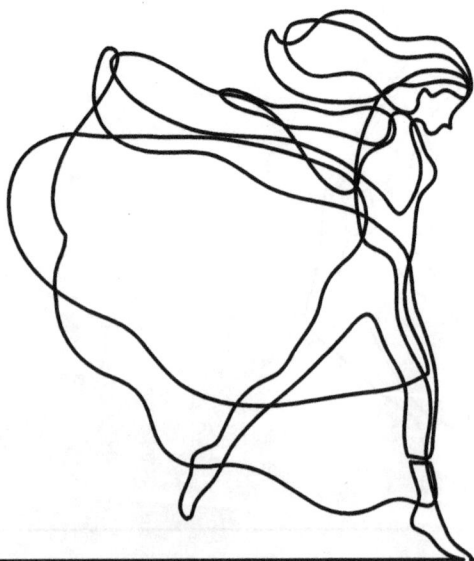

bodily remnants

God said
let my people twirl their fears away.

Sky falls with strain after such a wake of
flouted disscontempt.

Bodily remnants strewn amongst
the skipping stones for
camouflaged mortuary.

Looked Holiness direct from top to flare
curiosity burning depressions into relics through
thunderous provocation.

Heavenward

I surveyed the man who scaled a certain lip of tor

a slivered nail had snagged the edge of hull

rubbed wrong ways over a granite shelf.

Man grimaced before

hoisting palms heavenward for

God to salvage him from the sod and the brute

for a brief shake he ripened into a bird

sprung many shafts and exchanged homo sapient cage

for cavernous bones.

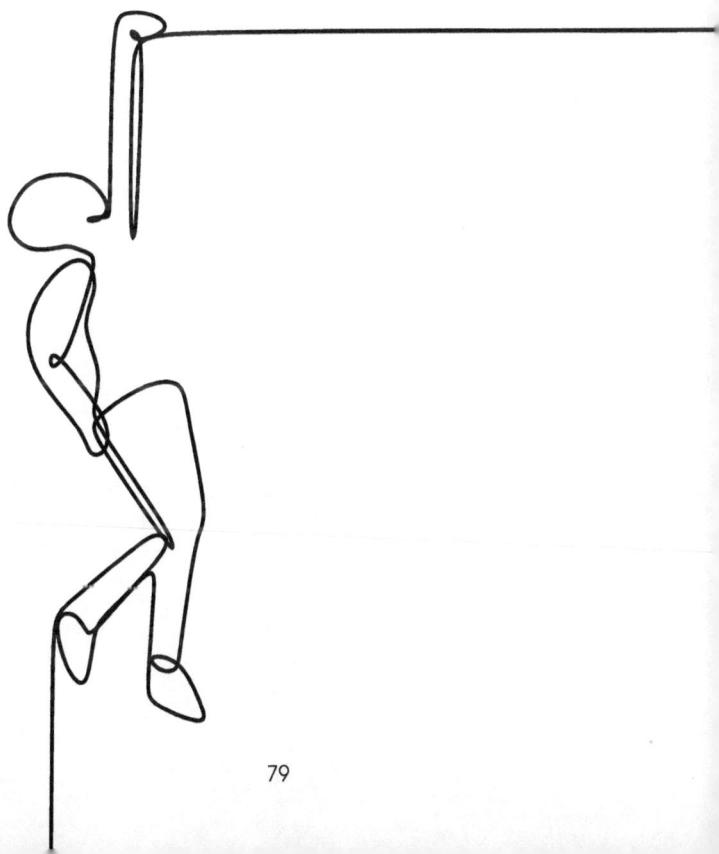

BERTH

Dear stars,

how were you completely swept into the cosmos
as bitty candle flies amidst
a fusillading kingdom of tears
memories of dead men
walking black and reckless
tears for their eight-year-old sons
who emerged as shovelers of winter's crest
tears for them who had to be
locks and stools to ward off the most obscure
guns for the prowler
who sank in waiting beyond
the campfire's trail of soot &
perhaps galileo wept you into effigies
       pain might have its rightful whereabouts

Acknowledgments

First and foremost, to my Lord and Savior for inspiring my words.

Thank you to my father who has taught me that whatever I do, I should do it with all my heart. I hope *Berth* is an act of obedience to your wisdom. To my mother who hasn't always understood the poems and their meaning, yet you care enough for me to ask the questions.

To Crystal Publishing for being *Berth's* home. Deanna Estes has made my dream come alive.

My gratitude to Malcolm Brooks for his encouragement and willingness to write the preface.

Thanks to my beta readers: Claire Richardson, Amy Behrendsen, and Dr. Lori Howe.

I wouldn't be where I am today without the brilliance of Kris Bigalk, Sun Yung Shin, John Reimringer, Dr. Lori Howe, and the countless other instructors and mentors who have encouraged me in the craft of writing.

And lastly, to the extraordinary writers, past and present, who have shown me the way: CS Lewis, JRR Tolkien, Ada Limon, Ross Gay, Ursula Le Guin, Tracy K Smith, Sara Eliz Johnson, and Malcolm Brooks, to name a few.

About the Author

From an early age, Megan Stratford was drawn to the outdoors. *Berth* is her poetic interpretation of nature, revealing her fascination and appreciation of the natural world. Stratford has an associate's degree from Normandale Community College, where she was encouraged to write poetry. Stratford was awarded the Patsy Lea Core in 2016. She placed second in the 2022 Wyoming Writers' category of free verse for her unique sense of style. She has published a small collection of poetry titled, *Espial* (Dancing Girl Press 2019). Her work also appears in the *North Dakota Quarterly, Shot Glass Journal, and Runestone*.

A native of Savage, Minnesota, Stratford currently resides in Sheridan, Wyoming, where she is a certified clinical massage therapist.

meganstratford.com

Continuous Line Drawing

Continuous line drawing is an artistic method whereby the drawing implement has uninterrupted contact with the surface of the paper. The image is a single, unbroken line. The medium is often used as an exercise for developing hand-eye coordination and observation skills.

First developed by Alexander Calder while he was a student at the Art Students League in New York City, simple line drawings have gained in popularity since they can be created in any environment and do not require a hefty time investment. Although any marking tool can be used, pens, markers, and graphite pencils are the most effective.

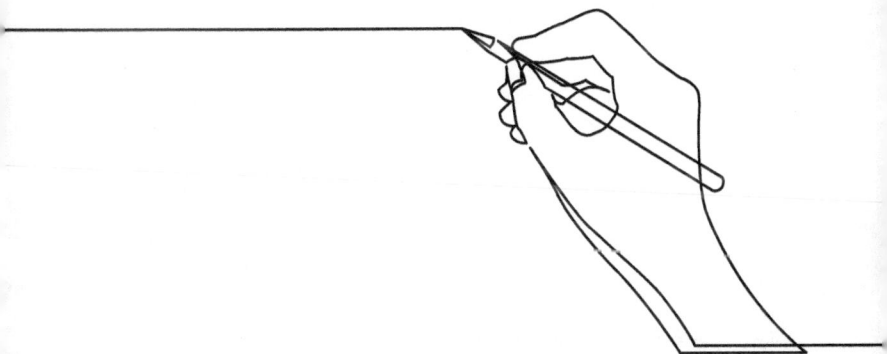

www.ingramcontent.com/pod-product-compliance
Lightning Source LLC
Chambersburg PA
CBHW022036090426
42741CB00007B/1091